MOOSE

A TRUE BOOK®

by

Ann O. Squire

Children's Press®
A Division of Scholastic Inc.

New York Toronto London Auckland Sydney
Mexico City New Delhi Hong Kong
Danbury, Connecticut

A road sign at a moose crossing

Content Consultant
Kathy Carlstead, PhD
*Research Scientist
Honolulu Zoo*

Reading Consultant
Cecilia Minden-Cupp, PhD
*Former Director, Language and
Literacy Program
Harvard Graduate School of
Education*

Author's Dedication
For Evan

*The photograph on the cover
shows a bull moose feeding in
a lake. The photograph on
the title page shows a bull
moose eating fireweed flowers
in the spring.*

Library of Congress Cataloging-in-Publication Data
Squire, Ann.
    Moose / by Ann O. Squire.
        p. cm. — (A True Book)
    Includes bibliographical references and index.
    ISBN-10: 0-516-25471-5 (lib. bdg.)   0-516-25582-7 (pbk.)
    ISBN-13: 978-0-516-25471-5 (lib. bdg.)   978-0-516-25582-8 (pbk.)
    1. Moose—Juvenile literature. I. Title. II. Series.
QL737.U55S69 2006
599.65'7—dc22   2005003288

CHILDREN'S PRESS, and A TRUE BOOK™, and associated logos are
trademarks and/or registered trademarks of Scholastic Library Publishing.
SCHOLASTIC and associated logos are trademarks and/or registered
trademarks of Scholastic Inc.
1 2 3 4 5 6 7 8 9 10 R 16 15 14 13 12 11 10 09 08 07   08

Contents

This male moose lives in Alaska's Denali National Park.

The Mighty Moose

If you've ever taken a drive in the country, you have probably seen deer grazing by the road or leaping off into the woods. But unless you've visited a zoo, you may never have seen the largest member of the deer family, the moose.

Moose are mostly solitary animals.

Moose are difficult to spot
for a few reasons. First, they
usually live in forests in the

most northern parts of the United States, Canada, Europe, and Asia. Second, moose are lone creatures that don't like to be bothered.

The most impressive thing about the moose is its size. Males, called **bulls**, can measure more than 6 feet (1.8 meters) from the hoof to the shoulder. They can weigh as much as 1,800 pounds (817 kilograms).

The moose's body is covered with thick fur that ranges from

reddish brown to almost black. The moose's legs are long. Broad hooves help it walk through wet mud or squishy swamps without sinking. The moose's head is huge, with a long, droopy snout.

Only the bulls have **antlers**. Atop the forehead of a bull is a pair of large, shovel-shaped antlers. While the antlers of other deer grow upward from the head, the antlers of moose grow out sideways.

Only the male moose have antlers (above). Moose have broad hooves and long snouts (left).

The bell is a flap of skin and hair that hangs under the moose's throat.

A moose's antlers can reach 6 feet (1.8 m) across. They can weigh more than 60 pounds (27 kg). The moose's neck must be thick and strong to support this weight.

Both males and females have a flap of skin and hair called a **bell** hanging underneath the throat. On a large bull moose, the bell can be as long as a person's arm. No one has ever determined what the bell is for.

Moose Munchies

Like many other animals, moose spend most of their waking hours looking for food. A moose needs to eat between 40 and 60 pounds (18 and 27 kg) of food every day to survive. Luckily, this animal likes many kinds of foods.

A moose's favorite foods are leaves and twigs. People believe

A bull moose chews on shrubs.

that the word *moose* comes from the American Indian words *mus* or *moos*, which mean "twig eater" or "he strips off bark." Moving through the forest, the moose munches on maple, aspen, willow, and dog-wood leaves. These trees are bare in the winter so the moose turns to balsam and fir, which keep their leaves throughout the year.

Because the moose is so tall, it can eat leaves and twigs

In the winter, moose feed on the leaves and twigs of evergreen trees.

that are too high for other animals to reach. Despite its great height, the moose also

Moose reach ground plants by spreading their front legs apart and leaning down.

manages to feed on plants on the ground. A moose's legs are too long and its neck is too short for it to eat ground plants while standing straight. So to reach low-growing plants and shrubs, the animal spreads its front legs apart, as giraffes do, and leans down. Moose will also kneel down to eat.

The moose has trouble bending over to take a drink. It usually solves this problem

Standing in the water is the easiest way for a moose to drink from a lake.

by wading into a river or lake. While there, the moose might feed on another favorite food, water lilies.

The moose is actually an excellent swimmer and a good diver. When a moose is searching for plants under the water,

A bull moose plunges into the water to find food.

Plants from the water provide the moose with salt.

it can dive as deep as 20 feet (6 m). It can stay underwater for forty seconds.

By winter's end, the moose's body craves salt. Munching water, or **aquatic**, plants is one way the moose gets the salt it needs. Some aquatic plants have four hundred times as much salt as the twigs that the moose eats during the winter. In the spring, the moose also looks for natural deposits in salt springs.

All About Antlers

When you look at a moose, what is the first thing you notice? You probably notice its antlers.

Like the antlers of other deer, a moose's antlers are made of solid bone. Unlike most bones, moose antlers grow very fast. They start as tiny knobs, called

Antlers grow on this young bull moose's head.

pedicels, on the moose's forehead and turn into fully grown antlers in only four months. What's even more amazing is that the moose grows a new pair of antlers each year.

Antlers are bulky and heavy for the moose to carry. But every male moose has antlers, so they must have a purpose. What is it? Like a lion's mane or a peacock's tail feathers, a moose's antlers are very important to winning a mate. In addition to showing off his impressive antlers, the male moose also uses them to battle other males.

In early spring, the two pedicels on the moose's forehead begin to grow. These small

antlers are covered with a
soft skin called the **velvet**.
As the summer wears on, the
antlers grow larger. They are
full-size by September.

A soft velvet
covers the
antlers of
this bull.

At this point, the antlers begin to harden. The velvet dries up and begins to peel off. The bull moose rubs his antlers against anything he can find to help remove the velvet. He also shoves other males and attacks trees and bushes to practice fighting.

In the fall, the males will use their antlers as weapons to fight for a mate. The males have no use for their antlers after mating. By December

A male sheds his velvet (above). Another bull tries to remove the velvet on a tree (right).

After mating, bulls shed their antlers.

or January, the antlers fall off by themselves. The males will be bareheaded until spring, when the antlers begin to grow all over again.

The Mating Game

For most of the year, moose are shy, quiet animals. All that changes in the fall. With his large, impressive pair of antlers, the bull moose is ready to find a female moose, or **cow**.

During mating season, the bull moose grows cross and impatient. He loses interest in food, and his eyes become red from lack of sleep. His only interest is in finding a mate. As he wanders through the forest, he moos loudly to let the females in the neighborhood know he is there. He may also dig a pit, urinate in it, and then roll around in it to attract females by smell.

Often a bull in search of a cow meets another male with the same idea. The bulls approach each other. They walk

Two bull moose spar during mating season.

stiff-legged, lower their heads, and raise the long hairs on the back of their necks. Suddenly, they charge, crashing their antlers together and trying to knock each other down.

If one bull is much larger than the other, the fight ends quickly and the loser runs away. But if the bulls are evenly matched, the battle may go on for hours. The fight scene looks like a disaster area, with bushes uprooted and trees knocked down.

When the fight is over, the winner mates with the cow, while the loser slinks away.

A bull and a cow greet each other.

Eight months later, the cow gives birth, usually to one **calf** or two calves. A new calf

A young moose calf crosses a stream.

weighs only about 25 to 30 pounds (11 to 14 kg). Its gangly legs seem much too long for its body. The calf will double its size in only three months.

By three weeks of age, the calf can follow its mother and

graze on leaves and twigs. The calf stays with its mother until it is one year old. At this time, the cow is ready to give birth again, and she drives her **yearling** away. Now the young moose is on its own.

These calves will stay with their mother until they are one year old.

Threats to Survival

Moose are huge, powerful animals. You might think that they have few enemies in the wild. In fact, grizzly bears and wolves hunt moose, especially sick or old ones. Moose calves are also a target. Scientists have found that bears kill half of the moose calves under eight weeks old.

A mother moose protects her calf from a young grizzly bear.

Adult moose also face threats to survival. In severe winters, many moose freeze to death or starve because of a lack of food.

Mad as a Moose

An angry moose is a dangerous animal, so it pays to know the warning signs. When a moose licks its lips, flattens its ears, and raises the long hairs on the back of its neck, watch out! Wildlife experts recommend running away as fast as possible. The moose probably won't chase you very far.

A bull moose

Two calves and their mother struggle against the winter cold.

Another threat is the winter tick, a tiny creature that burrows into the moose's skin and makes it itch. To relieve the itching, the moose rubs off some of the fur it needs for protection against the bitter winter cold.

Yet another threat is moose disease. Moose get this disease by accidentally swallowing tiny worms. An infected moose appears tame, walking around in circles until it finally collapses. Then it dies from lack of food or at the hands of a **predator**. The tiny worms can also kill the moose directly when the disease spreads to the brain.

People are responsible for the deaths of thousands of moose. Hunters as well as car, truck, and train accidents kill moose. As the number of humans in the Arctic increases, the problem is likely to grow.

A bull moose tries to cross a busy road in Anchorage, Alaska.

Sometimes human activities can help moose. When loggers cut down tall trees, smaller trees and shrubs that moose like to eat grow in their place. When managed fires burn in the forests, they clear thick forest growth. This allows the moose's favorite foods to grow.

As scientists study the effects of disease, predators, and human activities, they get a better idea of how to protect moose. With luck and some

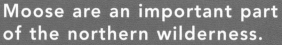

Moose are an important part of the northern wilderness.

work, these magnificent animals will always be a part of the northern wilderness.

To Find Out More

Here are some additional resources to help you learn more about moose:

 **Books**

DuTemple, Lesley A. **Moose**. Lerner Publications, 1998.

Fair, Jeff. **Moose Magic for Kids**. Gareth Stevens Publishing, 1995.

Fredericks, Anthony D. **Moose**. NorthWord Press, 2000.

Leach, Michael. **Moose: Habitats, Life Cycles, Food Chains, Threats**. Raintree, 2004.

Markert, Jenny. **Moose**. Child's World, 2000.

Organizations and Online Sites

Alaska Zoo
4731 O'Malley Road
Anchorage, AK 99507
907-346-2133
*http://www.alaskazoo.org/
index.htm*

The Alaska Zoo is home to almost one hundred birds and mammals, including many orphaned moose. Click on the "Virtual Tour" button to see an illustrated map of the zoo with links about all its animals.

Mooseworld
*http://www.mooseworld.
com/*

Look for photographs of moose in the wild, the latest news articles about moose, and some fun moose-related activities.

TheBigZoo.com
*http://www.thebigzoo.com/
Animals/Moose.asp*

Visit this site for moose photographs, quick moose facts, and more information about the largest member of the deer family.

Yellowstone National Park
PO Box 168
Yellowstone National
Park, WY 82190-0168
307-344-7381
*http://www.nps.gov/yell/
nature/animals/moose/
moose.html*

Check out this site to learn about the moose population at Yellowstone National Park. Consider visiting the park to see a moose in the wild for yourself.

45

Important Words

antlers the bony structures that grow from the foreheads of moose and other deer; a moose sheds its antlers every year

aquatic growing or living in the water

bell a flap of skin and hair that hangs under a moose's throat

bulls male moose

calf a baby moose

cow a female moose

pedicels small bumps on the forehead of a moose from which antlers grow

predator an animal that hunts and eats other animals

velvet the soft, blood-rich skin that envelops and nourishes the developing antlers of moose and other deer

yearling an animal that is one year old

Index

Meet the Author

Ann O. Squire has a PhD in animal behavior. Before becoming a writer, she spent several years studying African electric fish and the special signals they use to communicate with each other. Dr. Squire is the author of many books about natural science and animals, including *Beluga Whales*, *Lemmings*, *Penguins*, *Polar Bears*, and *Puffins*. She lives with her family in Katonah, New York.